A Picture Book of
George Washington

David A. Adler

illustrated by John & Alexandra Wallner

SCHOLASTIC INC.
New York Toronto London Auckland Sydney
Mexico City New Delhi Hong Kong

Titles in David A. Adler's *Picture Book* biography series:

A Picture Book of Abraham Lincoln
A Picture Book of Benjamin Franklin
A Picture Book of Christopher Columbus
A Picture Book of Eleanor Roosevelt
A Picture Book of George Washington
A Picture Book of Helen Keller
A Picture Book of Martin Luther King, Jr.
A Picture Book of Thomas Jefferson

ISBN 0-590-06772-9

 Published by Scholastic Inc., 555 Broadway, New York, NY 10012, by arrangement with Holiday House, Inc.

12 11 10 9 8 7 0 1 2/0

Printed in the U.S.A.

For Renée, with love.

D.A.A.

Thank you, Mr. Washington!

A.W. and J.W.

GEORGE WASHINGTON was born on February 22, 1732 in a simple Virginia farmhouse. At that time Virginia was an English colony.

Young George liked to fish and go boating. He watched ships that sailed past on the nearby river. But most of all he liked to ride his horse.

George learned to read and write in school. He practiced his handwriting by copying lists of rules such as "Keep your fingers clean" and "Think before you speak." But his favorite subject was arithmetic.

When George was eleven his father died. George helped his mother run their farm and watch his younger sister and brothers.

One day, George found some surveying tools that had belonged to his father. He used them to measure and map a turnip field and a pine forest. He liked surveying.

At sixteen George was very tall and looked much older. He was given a job surveying land in the Virginia wilderness.

In 1753, when George Washington was twenty-one, he joined the Virginia army. He rode to the Ohio Valley to warn the French to get off English land.

In 1754 the French and Indian War began. George Washington fought on the side of England. He led Virginia soldiers against the French. George was known as a brave and good leader throughout the thirteen American colonies.

When George was twenty-six he fell in love with Martha Custis. She was a wealthy widow with two children. They married and moved to Mount Vernon, the Virginia home and farm which once belonged to George's brother.

The English won their long war against the French. King George III of England wanted the American colonies to help pay the cost of the war, so he taxed them.

American colonists refused to pay the taxes. In Boston, colonists dumped tea into the harbor rather than pay the tax on it.

In April, 1775 fighting between England and her American colonies began near Boston, at Lexington and at Concord, Massachusetts. One month later leaders of the thirteen colonies met in Philadelphia. George Washington was chosen to lead the Continental Army.

Often there were not enough uniforms, food, blankets and guns for George Washington's soldiers.

The war lasted eight years. George Washington and the Continental Army fought bravely. In 1783, when the American colonies won the war, George Washington was a hero.

The thirteen colonies became thirteen states. They joined together and formed a government, but it was weak. In 1787 a new government was formed with a congress, a supreme court and a president. George Washington was the best-known, most loved leader in America. He was elected the first president of the United States of America in 1789. He was reelected in 1792.

President George Washington signed treaties with the Indians, Spain and England. There was a war in Europe, but George Washington kept the United States out of it. When some farmers in Pennsylvania refused to pay a tax on whiskey, George Washington sent soldiers to force the farmers to obey the law.

In 1797, after eight years as president, George Washington returned to his home at Mount Vernon.

Each morning he rode across his large farm on horseback.

Sometimes he rode fifteen miles north of Mount Vernon to watch the building of a new city. It would be the capital of the United States, and it would be named after him. It would be called Washington.

Then, in 1799 George Washington became ill and died. He was sixty-seven years old.

George Washington was a great leader. He has been called the "Father of Our Country." It has been said that George Washington was "First in war, first in peace and first in the hearts of his countrymen."

IMPORTANT DATES

1732	Born on February 22 in Virginia.
1755–1758	Was commander of the Virginia militia.
1759	Married Martha Custis on January 6.
1775–1783	Was commander in chief of the continental army.
1789	Was elected the first president of the United States.
1792	Was reelected president of the United States.
1796	Ended his second term as president.
1799	Died on December 14 at his Virginia home, Mount Vernon.